Guidance and mark schemes
Reading: Year 6

C000218743

Contents	Page
About this pack	4
Advice for parents and carers	5
Advice for children	6
Test coverage	6
Marking and assessing the papers	7
Marks table	7
Mark scheme for Test A	8
Mark scheme for Test B	12
Mark scheme for Test C	17

About this pack

This pack provides you with practice papers to help support children with the Key Stage 2 Reading test and to assess which skills need further development. The pack consists of this introductory booklet (including mark schemes) and three sample papers covering a wide range of content taken from the Key Stage 2 Programme of Study. A Reading booklet and answer booklet is provided for each paper.

Using the practice papers

The practice papers in this pack can be used as you would any other practice materials. The children will need to be familiar with specific test-focused skills, such as reading carefully, leaving questions until the end if they seem too difficult, working at a suitable pace and checking through their work.

If you choose to use the papers for looking at content rather than practising tests, do be aware of the time factor. The tests require a lot of work to be done in 1 hour as they are testing the degree of competence children have – it is not enough to be able to answer questions correctly but slowly.

About the tests

Each Reading test consists of texts covering different genres and contains 50 marks. Each test lasts for 1 hour, including reading time.

- Reading booklet: children may underline, highlight or make notes.
- Answer booklet: children should refer back to the reading booklet for their answers.

The marks available for each question are shown in the answer booklet next to each question and are also shown next to each answer in the mark scheme. Incorrect answers do not get a mark and no half marks should be given.

There are three different types of answer:

- **Selected answers**: children may be required to choose an option from a list; draw lines to match answers; or tick a correct answer. Usually 1 mark will be awarded.
- **Short answers**: children will need to write a phrase or use information from the text. Usually 1–2 marks will be awarded.
- **Several line answers**: children will need to write a sentence or two. Usually 1–2 marks will be awarded.
- **Longer answers**: children will usually need to write more than one sentence using information from the text. Up to 3 marks will be awarded.

YEAR 6
READING
National Curriculum Tests

Guidance and mark schemes

SCHOLASTIC

Scholastic Education, an imprint of Scholastic Ltd
Book End, Range Road, Witney, Oxfordshire, OX29 0YD
Registered office: Westfield Road, Southam,
Warwickshire CV47 0RA

www.scholastic.co.uk

© 2016 Scholastic Ltd

23456789 789012345

A British Library Cataloguing-in-Publication Data
A catalogue record for this book is available from the
British Library.

ISBN 978-1407-15913-3

Printed and bound in China by Hung Hing Offset Printing

Author
Graham Fletcher

Series consultants
Lesley and Graham Fletcher

Editorial team
Rachel Morgan, Tracey Cowell, Anna Hall,
Rebecca Rothwell, Shelley Welsh and Sally Rigg

Design team
Nicolle Thomas and Oxford Designers and Illustrators

Acknowledgements
Extracts from Department for Education website ©
Crown Copyright. Reproduced under the terms of the
Open Government Licence (OGL).
www.nationalarchives.gov.uk/doc/open-government-
licence/version/2/

Every effort has been made to trace copyright
holders for the works reproduced in this publication,
and the publishers apologise for any inadvertent
omissions.

Advice for parents and carers

How this pack will help

This pack will support your child to get ready for the KS2 National Reading tests commonly called SATs. It provides valuable practice and help on the responses and content expected of Year 6 children aged 10–11 years.

In the weeks (and sometimes months) leading up to the National Tests, your child will be given plenty of practice, revision and tips to give them the best possible chance to demonstrate their knowledge and understanding. It is important to try to practise outside of school and many children benefit from extra input. This pack will help your child prepare further and build their confidence and their ability to work to a time limit. Practice is vital and every opportunity helps, so don't start too late.

In this pack you will find three Reading tests. The layout and format of each test closely matches those used in the National Tests, so your child will become familiar with what to expect and get used to the style of the tests. In this booklet you will find a comprehensive answer section and guidance about how to mark the questions.

Tips

- Make sure that you allow your child to take the test in a quiet environment where they are not likely to be interrupted or distracted.

- Make sure your child has a flat surface to work on with plenty of space to spread out and good light.

- Emphasise the importance of reading and re-reading a question and to underline or circle any important information.

- These papers are similar to the one your child will take in May in Year 6 and they therefore give you a good idea of strengths and areas for development. So, when you have found areas that require some more practice, it is useful to go over these again and practise similar types of question with your child.

- Go through the tests again together, identify any gaps in learning and address any misconceptions or areas of misunderstanding. If you are unsure of anything yourself, then make an appointment to see your child's teacher who will be able to help and advise further.

Advice for children

What to do before the test

- Revise and practise on a regular basis.
- Spend some time each week practising.
- Focus on the areas you are least confident in to get better.
- Get a good night's sleep and eat a wholesome breakfast.
- Be on time for school.
- Have all the necessary materials.
- Avoid stressful situations before a test.

Test coverage

Children will need to be able to:

- Give and explain meanings of words.
- Find and copy key details.
- Summarise main ideas from more than one paragraph.
- Use details from the texts to explain their thoughts about them.
- Predict what might happen.
- Identify and explain how information is organised.
- Show how writers use language to create an effect.
- Make comparisons.

SCHOLASTIC Guidance and mark schemes

Marking and assessing the papers

The mark schemes and answers are located next in this booklet.

The mark schemes provide detailed examples of correct answers (although other variations/phrasings are often acceptable) and an explanation about what the answer should contain to be awarded a mark or marks.

Although the mark scheme sometimes contains alternative suggestions for correct answers, some children may find other ways of expressing a correct answer. When marking these tests, exercise judgement when assessing the accuracy or relevance of an answer and give credit for correct responses.

Marks table

At the back of each booklet there is a table for you to insert the number of marks achieved for each question. This will enable you to see which areas your child needs to practise further.

National Standard in Reading

The mark that your child gets in the test paper will be known as the 'raw score' (for example, '22' in 22/50). The raw score will be converted to a scaled score and children achieving a scaled score of 100 or more will achieve the National Standard in that subject. These 'scaled scores' enable results to be reported consistently year-on-year.

The guidance in the table below shows the marks that children need to achieve to reach the National Standard. This should be treated as a guide only, as the number of marks may vary. You can also find up-to-date information about scaled scores on our website: www.scholastic.co.uk/nationaltests

Marks achieved	Standard
0–20	Has not met the National Standard in Reading KS2
21–50	Has met the National Standard in Reading KS2

Mark scheme for Test A

Q	Answers	Marks
1	**Award 1 mark** for: little wolves.	1
2	**Award 1 mark** for answers such as: • It makes the reader feel like the passage is speaking directly to them • It makes the reader see the passage from the wolves' point of view	1
3	**Award 1 mark** for answers such as: • It makes it seem as if the wolf did nothing to the pigs. • The wolf doesn't deserve what happened to it.	1
4	**Award 1 mark** for: The most wanted criminals.	1
5	**Award 2 marks** for: • The wolves should avoid the pigs. • The wolves should make sure there is a large distance between them and the pigs. **Award 1 mark** for one of the above.	2
6	**Award 1 mark** for: A survival manual has been written.	1
7	**Award 1 mark** for answers that show understanding of the idea that the pigs look innocent and/or childlike but in reality are dangerous.	1
8	**Award 2 marks** for: • avoid contact • run away at once **Award 1 mark** for answers that include one of the above.	2
9	**Award 2 marks** for: • straw • sticks **Award 1 mark** for answers that include one of the above.	2
10	**Award 2 marks** for answers that suggest the pigs will come down the chimney and be boiled in the pan of water on the fire. **Award 1 mark** for answers that include one of the above.	2
11	**Award 1 mark** for: frightened at the beginning; happy at the end	1
12	**Award 2 marks** for full answers that include: • It gives advice on how to deal with pigs. • It makes it seem as if the pigs can be beaten. **Award 1 mark** for answers that include one of the above.	2
13	**Award 1 mark** for: • dangerous. • untrustworthy.	1
14	**Award 1 mark** for over fifty years.	1

SCHOLASTIC Guidance and mark schemes

Q	Answers	Marks
15	**Award I mark** for perhaps.	I
16	**Award I mark** for 75 miles.	I
17	**Award I mark** for all correct:	I

	Fact	Opinion
Blackpool and Southport are both in the north-west.	✓	
Blackpool is big and brash.		✓
Southport is more sedate.		✓
Blackpool and Southport both have wide expanses of golden sand.	✓	

Q	Answers	Marks
18	**Award 2 marks** for: • It is packed with mountains and magnificent views. • It has picture-postcard Christmas scenes. **Award I mark** for either of the above.	2
19	**Award I mark** for alliteration.	I
20	**Award 3 marks** for answers that include any of the following and a detailed explanation: • Nestling among them are chocolate-box villages that seem to have come straight out of history. • They are exactly what people think of when they picture English villages. • Some of them have romantic, almost ancient names like Bourton-on-the-Water, conjuring up images of days gone by. • Who could resist the mysteries suggested by the Slaughters, twin villages with a gruesome name? Detailed explanations could include, for example: • People might want to go to see the chocolate-box villages because they sound very attractive. • People who are interested in history might want to go to see the old villages. **Award 2 marks** for answers that include any of the above and some explanation. Explanations could include: • People might want to go to see the chocolate-box villages. • People who are interested in history might want to go. **Award I mark** for answers that include one sentence but do not give any explanation.	3
21	**Award 2 marks** for answers that include 'the bends are very tricky' and an explanation that refers to the quote. For example: If the readers are dreaming, they might crash because the bends are very tricky. **Award I mark** for answers that include 'the bends are very tricky' but do not give an explanation or answers that give an explanation but do not refer closely to the text.	2

Q	Answers	Marks
22	**Award 1 mark** for answers that indicate that there is a lot to do there.	1
23	**Award 3 marks** for answers that give a full explanation using evidence from all three downsides. For example: The writer tries to make the downsides seem unimportant by making them seem minor. The writer says it never rains long. The traffic can be heavy but the wait will be worth it. There is so much to do that you won't be able to choose. **Award 2 marks** for answers that explain but only use two examples. **Award 1 mark** for answers that give some explanation and an example.	3
24	**Award 1 mark** for answers that explain how the text would persuade. Answers must be text-specific. For example: The text tells the reader that you do not have to go abroad for good beaches **or** It gives the reader lots of choices of scenery or activity **or** It shows that there are no real drawbacks to holidays in England. **Do not accept** answers such as 'It sounds like a nice place' or 'It sounds interesting'.	1
25	**Award 1 mark** for Jerry. Accept Jeremiah.	1
26	**Award 1 mark** for any of the following: • He still had a proud way of holding his head and arching his neck. • He was a high-bred, fine-mannered, noble old horse, every inch of him. • He belonged to an officer in the cavalry and used to lead the regiment.	1
27	**Award 1 mark** for both correct: Polly and Dolly → talked in gentle voices. Polly and Dolly → petted Black Beauty.	1
28	**Award 1 mark** for 'difficult' or similar. **Do accept** 'tiring'.	1
29	**Award 1 mark** for any of the following: • It was a great treat to be petted again and talked to in a gentle voice • The broken knees • The 'Black Beauty' of olden times	1
30	**Award 1 mark** for make the horses more comfortable.	1
31	**Award 2 marks** for both of: • It chills a horse's stomach. • It spoils a horse's breathing. **Award 1 mark** for one of the above.	2

Q	Answers	Marks
32	**Award 1 mark** for any one of: • Captain was in the Crimean War. • Cabs are not pulled by horses nowadays. • There are carts and carriages on the streets in the story but we have cars and lorries.	1
33	**Award 1 mark** for animal welfare is important.	1
34	**Award 2 marks** for: • Jerry gave lots of clean water which he allowed to stand by them both day and night. **and** • Other grooms often went home to their beer, leaving the horses without water for hours. **Award 1 mark** for an answer that includes some of the above but does not compare.	2
35	**Award 1 mark** for Captain's story is mentioned in both paragraphs	1
36	**Award 2 marks** for any two of: • Captain went to the Crimean War. • He belonged to an officer in the cavalry. • He used to lead the regiment. **Award 1 mark** for any one of the above.	2

Mark scheme for Test B

Q	Answers	Marks
1	**Award 1 mark** for answers that suggest boring, tedious, slow or similar.	1
2	**Award 1 mark** for: • What a let-down • there seemed little of interest	1
3	**Award 1 mark** for 'He had never been allowed' or 'This was forbidden territory'.	1
4	**Award 1 mark** for answers that recognise why the feature is used. Possible responses: • It makes you wonder what could happen and want to know the answer. • It builds tension. • It makes the reader feel how much James wants to know what is in the chest.	1
5	**Award 1 mark** for 'struggled', 'groped' or similar. The answer must show some understanding of James not finding it easy to open the chest.	1
6	**Award 2 marks** for answers that show a full understanding of the simile. Possible response: • The dust is likened to small planets floating in space. This helps the reader understand what the dust looked like because the pieces of dust seem very small in the space of the room. **Award 1 mark** for answers that show a general understanding of the use of figurative language. Possible responses: • It paints a picture that the reader can see. • It helps the reader to understand what the dust looked like.	2
7	**Award 1 mark** for a reasonable inference. Possible responses: • It is the only place to hide. • He is trying to hide from his father. • The voice tells him to do it. • He panics.	1
8	**Award 1 mark** for a ventriloquist's dummy.	1
9	**Award 1 mark** for answers that indicate that James' father thinks he has caught whoever/whatever is in the tower.	1
10	**a. Award 1 mark** for answers that include James, an intruder or similar.	1
	b. Award 1 mark for answers that include 'He was sure he had heard movement and voices' or 'The only hiding place!'	1

SCHOLASTIC Guidance and mark schemes

Q	Answers	Marks
11	**Award 2 marks** for answers that identify two events. Possible responses: • James opening the chest. • James being surprised by his father's voice at the bottom of the stairs. • James's father coming up the stairs. • When James first hears the voice in the chest. • James's father seeing the chest. • The chest being empty when James's father opens it. **Award 1 mark** for answers that only include one event.	2
12	**Award 1 mark** for answers that show the link between magic and James disappearing.	1
13	**a. Award 1 mark** for any likely answer. Possible responses: • He will continue looking for James. • He will give up looking for James. **b. Award 1 mark** for a reason that is supported by the text. Possible responses: • He is worried about where James might be and wants to find him because he sounded 'anxious'. • He thinks that he must have been mistaken about hearing something in the bell tower.	1 1
14	**Award 1 mark** for all correct: <table><tr><td>James hears a voice coming from the chest.</td><td>5</td></tr><tr><td>James climbs the bell tower.</td><td>1</td></tr><tr><td>James puts on the cloak.</td><td>3</td></tr><tr><td>James opens the chest.</td><td>2</td></tr><tr><td>James's father opens the chest.</td><td>6</td></tr><tr><td>James's father calls to James.</td><td>4</td></tr></table>	1
15	**Award 1 mark** for handsome.	1
16	**Award 1 mark** for answers that show understanding of the writer's opposition to pirates. Possible responses: • It tells us the writer wishes pirates did not exist now. • The writer thinks pirates are a bad thing.	1

Q	Answers	Marks
17	**Award 1 mark** for answers that include one of the following. Possible responses: • They are ruthless. • They are not romantic. • They are not funny – don't tell jokes, don't talk Pirate. • They don't wear pirate outfits – striped T-shirts, eye patches, wooden legs. • They use speed boats, rifles and rocket-propelled grenades. • They attack all kinds of ships.	1
18	**a. Award 1 mark** for: The coasts of Somalia.	1
	b. Award 1 mark for answers that give reasons. Possible responses: • Somalia is a poor country. • The pirates used to be fishermen but cannot catch fish any longer.	1
19	**Award 1 mark** for all correct: Many pirates used to be → fishermen. Successful pirates are → rich and live well. Accountants manage the → money of some pirates. In poor countries piracy is seen as → a business activity.	1
20	**Award 3 marks** for answers that include three of the following: • Pirates are taking hostages and demanding ransoms rather than just taking cargoes. • Pirates are being forced into more open water, away from the coast. • Piracy is reducing. • There is more piracy off the west coast of Africa now than off Somalia. **Award 2 marks** for answers that include two of the above. **Award 1 mark** for answers that include one of the above.	3
21	**Award 1 mark** for answers that explain that international patrols have made it more difficult for pirates to operate.	1
22	**Award 3 marks** for answers that include any three of: • *Captain Phillips* shows a more realistic view of piracy. • The events are seen from the victim's (Captain Phillips's) point of view, which is different to before. • Hollywood has made the captain the hero, not the pirates. • Earlier films were romantic/glamorised and showed events from the pirates' point of view. • Previously, Hollywood made the pirates look handsome, good-hearted and heroic. This film shows the horror of an attack. **Award 2 marks** for answers that include two of the above responses. **Award 1 mark** for answers that include one of the above responses.	3

SCHOLASTIC Guidance and mark schemes

Q	Answers	Marks
23	**Award I mark** for all correct:	I

	Fact	Opinion
It is easy to see why, in a poor country, piracy is seen not so much as a crime but as a legitimate business activity.		✓
For the first time, in 2012, Somali pirate attacks dropped.	✓	
Captain Phillips is based on the true story of the unarmed American cargo vessel *Maersk Alabama*.	✓	
However, if it does not make a lot of money, you can be sure that Hollywood will revert back to the buccaneers.		✓

Q	Answers	Marks
24	**Award 2 marks** for answers that include: • Pirates are popular in cinemas. • Pirate films make lots of money. **Award I mark** for answers that include one of the above.	2
25	**Award I mark** for a container of water or similar.	I
26	**Award I mark** for answers that show that he was afraid of the snake and did not want to disturb it.	I
27	**Award I mark** for yellow-brown. Accept gold.	I
28	**Award 2 marks** for answers that include two of the following: • It moved slowly. • It was soft-skinned. • It was thirsty. • It was beautiful. • It was brightly-coloured. **Award I mark** for answers that include one of the above.	2
29	**Award I mark** for answers that show that the snake was venomous/ poisonous/dangerous.	I
30	**Award I mark** for answers that include killing the snake with a stick or beating it to death or similar. **Do not award marks** for answers that just copy the text.	I
31	**a. Award I mark** for 'If you were a man'.	I
	b. Award I mark for answers that suggest the writer would be weak if he didn't do it.	I
32	**Award 2 marks** for any two of: • The writer liked the snake. • He was glad he had seen it. • He felt honoured to have seen it. **Award I mark** for one of the above.	2

Q	Answers		Marks
33	**Award 1 mark** for all correct:		1

The snake leaves.	4
The writer sees the snake.	1
The snake looks at the writer.	3
The snake drinks.	2
The writer feels honoured.	5

Q	Answers	Marks
34	**Award 3 marks** for answers that include all of the following: • I must confess how I liked him • How glad I was he had come • I felt so honoured **Award 2 marks** for answers that include two of the above. **Award 1 mark** for answers that include one of the above.	3
35	**Award 1 mark** for answers that indicate that the reader tries to answer the questions.	1

SCHOLASTIC Guidance and mark schemes

Mark scheme for Test C

Q	Answers	Marks
1	**Award 1 mark** for: She would get a bike.	1
2	**Award 1 mark** for: sister.	1
3	**Award 1 mark** for answers that show the connection between Minnie and Mouse – Minnie Mouse.	1
4	**Award 2 marks** for answers that include: ● She was expecting a bike. ● The skates weren't even inline ones. **Award 1 mark** for answers that include one of the above.	2
5	**Award 1 mark** for her gran or Gran.	1
6	**Award 2 marks** for answers that include: ● Get up early on Christmas Day. ● Kiss her father. **Award 1 mark** for answers that include one of the above.	2
7	**Award 2 marks** for: ● The spokes look like the strings of a harp. ● The bent wheel could look like the shape of a harp. **Award 1 mark** for answers that include one of the above.	2
8	**Award 3 marks** for full answers that include at least three of: ● Every time the trumpet appears, it causes trouble. ● The trumpet is used to annoy the writer. ● The writer gets into trouble for putting the trumpet in the bin. ● The trumpet is retrieved from the bin only for the writer's father to put it back again. **Award 2 marks** for answers that include at least two of the above. **Award 1 mark** for answers that include at least one of the above.	3
9	**Award 1 mark** for Minnie had played Jingle Bells 24 times without a break and this was too much for her father.	1
10	**Award 1 mark** for four.	1
11	**Award 1 mark** for The worst Christmas ever.	1
12	**a. Award 1 mark** for answers that explain it has times, or it goes through the events of the day in order.	1
	b. Award 1 mark for answers that explain it makes it easy to follow the events of the day, or it makes it easy to understand the writer's changing attitude.	1

Q	Answers	Marks
13	**Award 3 marks** for full answers that include reasons for the changing attitudes. Possible response: • Before Christmas Day, the writer thinks this will be the best Christmas ever because she is going to get a bike. This changes on Christmas Day when her sister wakes her up at six o'clock and she is given roller skates. It becomes the best Christmas again when she gets the bike. It continues because Minnie is grounded. It finally becomes the worst Christmas again when the writer crashes the bike. **Award 2 marks** for answers that recognise some changes and give reasons. Possible response: • Before Christmas Day, the writer thinks this will be the best Christmas ever because she is going to get a bike. This changes on Christmas Day when she is given roller skates. It becomes the best Christmas again when she gets the bike. It finally becomes the worst Christmas again when the writer crashes the bike. **Award 1 mark** for answers that recognise the overall change in attitude. Possible response: • The writer's attitude changes from it being the best Christmas at the start to the worst at the end.	3
14	**Award 1 mark** for: • Hokkaido • Honshu • Shikoku • Kyushu. Do not penalise for spelling as long as the intention is clear.	1
15	**Award 1 mark** for: • a hot, damp summer • a cooler, drier winter.	1
16	**Award 1 mark** for mostly.	1
17	**a. Award 1 mark** for August.	1
	b. Award 1 mark for January.	1
18	**Award 2 marks** for answers that include the following and compare: • the north: the winters are long and cold • the Pacific coast: has milder winters with little snow. **Award 1 mark** for answers that only contain one of the above or do not compare.	2
19	**Award 1 mark** for: • electronics • cars • motorcycles.	1

Q	Answers	Marks
20	**Award 2 marks** for answers that include two of the following and compare: • Japan's rugby team is more successful than the football team. • The rugby team is the most successful in Asia. • The rugby team has won the Asia Five Nations competition six times. • The football team has reached the final stages of the FIFA World Cup. • The football team co-hosted the FIFA World Cup in 2002. **Award 1 mark** for answers that include two of the above but do not compare, or answers that include one of the above and compare.	2
21	**Award 2 marks** for a correct fact and a correct opinion. For example: • Fact: Japan's flag is the Rising Sun. • Opinion: its future seems bright. **Award 1 mark** for a correct fact or a correct opinion.	2
22	**Award 1 mark** for all four pairs matched correctly.	1

Q	Answers	Marks
23	**Award 1 mark** for In a geography textbook.	1
24	**Award 1 mark** for A snapshot of Japan.	1
25	**Award 1 mark** for morning.	1
26	**Award 1 mark** for grey.	1
27	**Award 1 mark** for a ship.	1
28	**Award 2 marks** for answers that give both an interpretation and an example. Possible responses: • The author shows that the sea was rough by saying that the 'ship was rolling in the ocean swell'. • He describes how the sea is making the boat move suddenly: 'jumping like an injured animal'. • The author describes the noises the boat is making to tell us that the sea is moving it: 'The rudder was banging to and fro' and 'the whole ship was creaking, groaning'. • Jim tells us that he is being thrown around in the boat so the sea must be rough: 'I had to cling on tight to the rope'. • The main character is being 'rolled about like a bottle' which tells us the boat is moving from side to side. **Award 1 mark** for answers that include either an explanation or an example but not both.	2
29	**Award 1 mark** for answers that suggest either of the following or similar: • The ship seemed as light as a bottle on the sea. • The ship had no control over itself.	1

Q	Answers	Marks
30	**Award I mark** for answers that show an understanding of the author's feeling of depression, fear or sadness.	I
31	**Award I mark** for any of the following quotations: • The men grumbled fiercely. • The very sight of the island seemed to have made them give up working. • If the behaviour of the men had been alarming in the boat, it became truly threatening when they had come back on board the *Hispaniola*. • They lay about the deck growling together in talk. • The slightest order was received with a black look and grudgingly and carelessly obeyed. • Mutiny, it was plain, hung over us like a thunder cloud.	I
32	**Award I mark** for except or words of similar meaning.	I
33	**Award I mark** for the island is an unhealthy place to go.	I
34	**Award I mark** for answers that indicate some sort of mutiny/rebellion will happen or that Long John will be overthrown.	I
35	**Award I mark** for rebellion.	I
36	**Award I mark** for to find the treasure.	I
37	**Award I mark** for answers that give a reason for the use of the first-person narrator. Possible responses: • To help us understand the character's point of view. • To make events seem more real. • To show us how the main character feels. • To make us feel as though the events are happening to us. • To make us feel that someone is telling a story of what happened to them. • To make us feel that the story is true.	I